interchange
FIFTH EDITION

Workbook

Jack C. Richards

intro A

CAMBRIDGE UNIVERSITY PRESS

CAMBRIDGE
UNIVERSITY PRESS & ASSESSMENT

Shaftesbury Road, Cambridge CB2 8EA, United Kingdom

One Liberty Plaza, 20th Floor, New York, NY 10006, USA

477 Williamstown Road, Port Melbourne, VIC 3207, Australia

314–321, 3rd Floor, Plot 3, Splendor Forum, Jasola District Centre, New Delhi – 110025, India

103 Penang Road, #05–06/07, Visioncrest Commercial, Singapore 238467

Cambridge University Press & Assessment is a department of the University of Cambridge.

We share the University's mission to contribute to society through the pursuit of education, learning and research at the highest international levels of excellence.

www.cambridge.org
Information on this title: www.cambridge.org/9781316622391

© Cambridge University Press & Assessment 1994, 2017

This publication is in copyright. Subject to statutory exception and to the provisions of relevant collective licensing agreements, no reproduction of any part may take place without the written permission of Cambridge University Press & Assessment.

First published 1994
Second edition 2000
Third edition 2005
Fourth edition 2013
Fifth edition 2017
Fifth edition update published 2021

20 19 18 17 16 15 14 13 12 11 10 9 8 7

Printed in Poland by Opolgraf

A catalogue record for this publication is available from the British Library

ISBN 978-1-009-04041-9 Intro Student's Book with eBook
ISBN 978-1-009-04042-6 Intro Student's Book A with eBook
ISBN 978-1-009-04043-3 Intro Student's Book B with eBook
ISBN 978-1-009-04055-6 Intro Student's Book with Digital Pack
ISBN 978-1-009-04056-3 Intro Student's Book A with Digital Pack
ISBN 978-1-009-04057-0 Intro Student's Book B with Digital Pack
ISBN 978-1-316-62237-7 Intro Workbook
ISBN 978-1-316-62239-1 Intro Workbook A
ISBN 978-1-316-62240-7 Intro Workbook B
ISBN 978-1-108-40605-5 Intro Teacher's Edition
ISBN 978-1-316-62221-6 Intro Class Audio
ISBN 978-1-009-04058-7 Intro Full Contact with Digital Pack
ISBN 978-1-009-04059-4 Intro Full Contact A with Digital Pack
ISBN 978-1-009-04062-4 Intro Full Contact B with Digital Pack
ISBN 978-1-108-40304-7 Presentation Plus Intro

Additional resources for this publication at cambridgeone.org

Cambridge University Press & Assessment has no responsibility for the persistence or accuracy of URLs for external or third-party internet websites referred to in this publication and does not guarantee that any content on such websites is, or will remain, accurate or appropriate.

Contents

	Credits	iv
1	What's your name?	1
2	Where are my keys?	7
3	Where are you from?	13
4	Is this coat yours?	19
5	What time is it?	25
6	I ride my bike to school.	31
7	Does it have a view?	37
8	Where do you work?	43

Credits

The authors and publishers acknowledge the following sources of copyright material and are grateful for the permissions granted. While every effort has been made, it has not always been possible to identify the sources of all the material used, or to trace all copyright holders. If any omissions are brought to our notice, we will be happy to include the appropriate acknowledgements on reprinting and in the next update to the digital edition, as applicable.

Key: B = Below, BC = Below Centre, BL = Below Left, BR = Below Right, C = Centre, CL = Centre Left, CR = Centre Right, Ex = Exercise, L = Left, R = Right, T = Top, TC = Top Centre, TL = Top Left, TR = Top Right.

Illustrations

337 Jon (KJA Artists): 11, 21, 81; **417 Neal** (KJA Artists): 1, 58; **Mark Duffin**: 7, 12, 26, 37, 41, 52, 70; **Thomas Girard** (Good Illustration): 10, 63, 68, 84; **John Goodwin** (Eye Candy Illustration): 23, 71; **Dusan Lakicevic** (Beehive Illustration): 57; **Quino Marin** (The Organisation): 19, 69, 92, 94; **Gavin Reece** (New Division): 5, 39; **Gary Venn** (Lemonade Illustration): 25, 74, 77; **Paul Williams** (Sylvie Poggio Artists): 6, 29, 67.

Photos

Back cover (woman with whiteboard): Jenny Acheson/Stockbyte/GettyImages; Back cover (whiteboard): Nemida/GettyImages; Back cover (man using phone): Betsie Van Der Meer/Taxi/GettyImages; Back cover (woman smiling): PeopleImages.com/DigitalVision/GettyImages; Back cover (name tag): Tetra Images/GettyImages; Back cover (handshake): David Lees/Taxi/GettyImages; p. 2 (TL): Yellow Dog Productions/Iconica/GettyImages; p. 2 (CR): Morsa Images/DigitalVision/GettyImages; p. 2 (BL): Johnny Greig/iStock/Getty Images Plus/GettyImages; p. 3: Nicolas McComber/E+/GettyImages; p. 4: MichaelDeLeon/iStock/Getty Images Plus/GettyImages; p. 5: Steve Debenport/E+/GettyImages; p. 8 (TL): hudiemm/E+/GettyImages; p. 8 (TC): Marek Mnich/E+/GettyImages; p. 8 (TR): Dorling Kindersley/Dorling Kindersley/GettyImages; p. 8 (CL): Tpopova/iStock/Getty Images Plus/GettyImages; p. 8 (C): Tpopova/iStock/Getty Images Plus/GettyImages; p. 8 (CR): Creative Crop/DigitalVision/GettyImages; p. 8 (BR): Betsie Van Der Meer/Taxi/GettyImages; p. 9 (TR): michaeljung/iStock/Getty Images Plus/GettyImages; p. 9 (B): Milk & Honey Creative/Stockbyte/GettyImages; p. 13: Martin Barraud/OJO Images/GettyImages; p. 14 (TL): Lumina Images/Blend Images/GettyImages; p. 14 (TR): Elyse Lewin/Photographer's Choice/GettyImages; p. 14 (BL): Fabrice LEROUGE/ONOKY/GettyImages; p. 14 (BR): Susan Chiang/iStock/Getty Images Plus/GettyImages; p. 15 (TL): franckreporter/E+/GettyImages; p. 15 (TR): AWL Images/AWL Images/GettyImages; p. 15 (CL): Image Source/Image Source/GettyImages; p. 15 (CR): Matthias Tunger/Photolibrary/GettyImages; p. 15 (BL): MATTES RenÃ©/hemis.fr/hemis.fr/GettyImages; p. 15 (BR): Luis Davilla/Photolibrary/GettyImages; p. 16: Bruce Glikas/FilmMagic/GettyImages; p. 17 (TL): Digital Vision/Digital Vision/GettyImages; p. 17 (CL): Thomas Barwick/Iconica/GettyImages; p. 17 (C): skynesher/E+/GettyImages; p. 17 (BC): Hans Neleman/The Image Bank/GettyImages; p. 17 (BL): RunPhoto/Photodisc/GettyImages; p. 17 (CR): Portra Images/Taxi/GettyImages; p. 17 (BR): Terry Vine/Blend Images/GettyImages; p. 18: Jupiterimages/Stockbyte/GettyImages; p. 20: Hero Images/Hero Images/GettyImages; p. 22 (TL): Gabriela Tulian/Moment/GettyImages; p. 22 (TR): James A. Guilliam/Photolibrary/GettyImages; p. 22 (CL): Stuart Stevenson photography/Moment/GettyImages; p. 22 (CR): Cultura RM Exclusive/Stephen Lux/Cultura Exclusive/GettyImages; p. 22 (BL): Robert Daly/Caiaimage/GettyImages; p. 22 (BR): noelbesuzzi/RooM/GettyImages; p. 24 (TL): Tim Robberts/Taxi/GettyImages; p. 24 (TR): Jan Scherders/Blend Images/GettyImages; p. 24 (BL): Chris Whitehead/Cultura/GettyImages; p. 24 (BR): A J James/Photodisc/GettyImages; p. 26: Paul Bradbury/Caiaimage/GettyImages; p. 27 (TL): Caiaimage/Trevor Adeline/Caiaimage/GettyImages; p. 27 (TC): Hero Images/Hero Images/GettyImages; p. 27 (TR): Westend61//GettyImages; p. 27 (CL): Susan Chiang/E+/GettyImages; p. 27 (C): shapecharge/E+/GettyImages; p. 27 (CR): Image Source/Image Source/GettyImages; p. 27 (BL): Henrik Sorensen/Iconica/GettyImages; p. 27 (BC): Hero Images/Hero Images/GettyImages; p. 27 (BR): Dougal Waters/DigitalVision/GettyImages; p. 28 (Ex 6.1): Hoxton/Tom Merton/Hoxton/GettyImages; p. 28 (Ex 6.2): Mike Harrington/The Image Bank/GettyImages; p. 28 (Ex 6.3): Alexander Rhind/Stone/GettyImages; p. 28 (Ex 6.4): Vico Collective/Alin Dragulin/Blend Images/GettyImages; p. 28 (Ex 6.5): Leonardo Patrizi/E+/GettyImages; p. 28 (Ex 6.6): JGI/Tom Grill/Blend Images/GettyImages; p. 28 (Ex 6.7): elenaleonova/iStock/Getty Images Plus/GettyImages; p. 28 (Ex 6.8): Thomas Barwick/Iconica/GettyImages; p. 30: Tetra Images/Tetra Images/GettyImages; p. 31 (TL): Caiaimage/Sam Edwards/Caiaimage/GettyImages; p. 31 (TR): Shestock/Blend Images/GettyImages; p. 31 (C): Marc Romanelli/Blend Images/GettyImages; p. 32: Dave & Les Jacobs/Blend Images/Getty Images Plus/GettyImages; p. 33: Dan Porges/Photolibrary/GettyImages; p. 33: Sam Edwards/Caiaimage/GettyImages; p. 34: Hero Images/Hero Images/GettyImages; p. 35: Hero Images/Hero Images/GettyImages; p. 36: XiXinXing/XiXinXing/GettyImages; p. 38: Mint Images - Tim Robbins/Mint Images RF/GettyImages; p. 40 (T): Klaus Tiedge/Blend Images/GettyImages; p. 40 (B): nwinter/iStock/Getty Images Plus/GettyImages; p. 43 (Ex 1a): Daniel Allan/Photographer's Choice/GettyImages; p. 43 (Ex 1b): Gary John Norman/Iconica/GettyImages; p. 43 (Ex 1c): Paul Bradbury/Caiaimage/GettyImages; p. 43 (Ex 1d): Dave and Les Jacobs/Lloyd Dobbie/Blend Images/GettyImages; p. 43 (Ex 1e): Hero Images/Hero Images/GettyImages; p. 43 (Ex 1f): BJI/Blue Jean Images/GettyImages; p. 43 (Ex 1g): XiXinXing/GettyImages; p. 43 (Ex 1h): Phil Boorman/Cultura/GettyImages; p. 43 (Ex 1i): Gary John Norman/The Image Bank/GettyImages; p. 43 (Ex 1j): Cultura RM Exclusive/yellowdog/Cultura Exclusive/GettyImages; p. 44 (Ex 2.1): Portra Images/Taxi/GettyImages; p. 44 (Ex 2.2): Paper Boat Creative/DigitalVision/GettyImages; p. 44 (Ex 2.3): Monty Rakusen/Cultura/GettyImages; p. 44 (Ex 2.4): Hero Images/Stone/GettyImages; p. 44 (Ex 2.5): diego_cervo/iStock/Getty Images Plus/GettyImages; p. 44 (Ex 2.6): Caiaimage/Robert Daly/OJO+/GettyImages; p. 45 (TL): Jetta Productions/Iconica/GettyImages; p. 45 (TR): Dana Neely/Stone/GettyImages; p. 45 (BL): Rob Daly/OJO Images/GettyImages; p. 45 (BR): vgajic/E+/GettyImages; p. 46 (T): Hero Images/Hero Images/GettyImages; p. 46 (B): zoranm/E+/GettyImages; p. 47 (T): HAYKIRDI/iStock/Getty Images Plus/GettyImages; p. 47 (B): onepony/iStock/Getty Images Plus/GettyImages; p. 48 (Ex 6.1): Klaus Vedfelt/Taxi/GettyImages; p. 48 (Ex 6.2): Caiaimage/Sam Edwards/Caiaimage/GettyImages; p. 48 (Ex 6.3): Inti St Clair/Blend Images/GettyImages; p. 48 (Ex 6.4): Monty Rakusen/Cultura/GettyImages; p. 48 (Ex 6.5): JGI/Tom Grill/Blend Images/GettyImages; p. 48 (Ex 6.6): Caiaimage/Tom Merton/Caiaimage/GettyImages; p. 49 (Ex 1.1): Rosemary Calvert/Photographer's Choice/GettyImages; p. 49 (Ex 1.2): Bruno Crescia Photography Inc/First Light/GettyImages; p. 49 (Ex 1.3): Roger Dixon/Dorling Kindersley/GettyImages; p. 49 (Ex 1.4): Alexander Bedrin/iStock/Getty Images Plus/GettyImages; p. 49 (Ex 1.5): Kaan Ates/iStock/Getty Images Plus/GettyImages; p. 49 (Ex 1.6): David Marsden/Photolibrary/GettyImages; p. 49 (Ex 1.7): RedHelga/E+/GettyImages; p. 49 (Ex 1.8): rimglow/iStock/Getty Images Plus/GettyImages; p. 49 (Ex 1.9): Suwanmanee99/iStock/Getty Images Plus/GettyImages; p. 49 (Ex 1.10): Creative Crop/DigitalVision/GettyImages; p. 49 (Ex 1.11): Dorling Kindersley/Dorling Kindersley/GettyImages; p. 49 (Ex 1.12): mm88/iStock/Getty Images Plus/GettyImages; p. 49 (Ex 1.13): kbwills/iStock/Getty Images Plus/GettyImages; p. 49 (Ex 1.14): Steve Wisbauer/Photolibrary/GettyImages; p. 49 (Ex 1.15): Tomas_Mina/iStock/Getty Images Plus/GettyImages; p. 49 (Ex 1.16): Freila/iStock/Getty Images Plus/GettyImages; p. 49 (Ex 1.17): Paul Poplis/Photolibrary/GettyImages; p. 49 (Ex 1.18): Dorling Kindersley/Dorling Kindersley/GettyImages; p. 49 (Ex 1.19): Science Photo Library/Science Photo Library/GettyImages; p. 49 (Ex 1.20): Gary Sergraves/Dorling Kindersley/GettyImages; p. 50 (Ex 2.1): Dave King Dorling Kindersley/Dorling Kindersley/GettyImages; p. 50 (Ex 2.2): fcafotodigital/E+/GettyImages; p. 50 (Ex 2.3): Susan Trigg/E+/GettyImages; p. 50 (Ex 2.4): Davies and Starr/The Image Bank/GettyImages; p. 50 (Ex 2.5): Kai Schwabe/StockFood Creative/GettyImages; p. 50 (Ex 2.6): Kevin Summers/Photographer's Choice/GettyImages; p. 50 (Ex 3.1): 109508Liane Riss/GettyImages; p. 51 (T): Digital Vision/Photodisc/GettyImages; p. 51 (B): Lisa Hubbard/Photolibrary/GettyImages; p. 53 (T): MIXA/GettyImages; p. 53 (B): Tom Grill/The Image Bank/GettyImages; p. 54: Jake Curtis/Iconica/GettyImages; p. 55 (Ex 1a): Shell_114/iStock/Getty Images Plus/GettyImages; p. 55 (Ex 1b): C Squared Studios/Photodisc/GettyImages; p. 55 (Ex 1c): Image Source/ Image Source/GettyImages; p. 55 (Ex 1d): inxti/iStock/Getty Images Plus/GettyImages; p. 55 (Ex 1e): skodonnell/E+/GettyImages; p. 55 (Ex 1f): by_nicholas/E+/GettyImages; p. 55 (Ex 1g): koosen/iStock/Getty Images Plus/GettyImages; p. 55 (Ex 1h): Creativ Studio Heinemann/GettyImages; p. 55 (Ex 1i): Lazi & Mellenthin/GettyImages; p. 55 (Ex 1j): stockbymh/iStock/Getty Images Plus/GettyImages; p. 56 (T): John P Kelly/The Image Bank/GettyImages; p. 56 (B): Nicola Tree/The Image Bank/GettyImages; p. 59 (T): Zave Smith/Photolibrary/GettyImages; p. 59 (C): XiXinXing/GettyImages; p. 59 (B): Steve Mcsweeny/Moment/GettyImages; p. 60: Dougal Waters/Taxi/GettyImages; p. 61 (spring): Maria Viola/EyeEm/EyeEm/GettyImages; p. 61 (summer): Dothan Nareswari/EyeEm/EyeEm/GettyImages; p. 61 (fall): Plattform/GettyImages; p. 61 (winter): juliannafunk/iStock/Getty Images Plus/GettyImages; p. 64 (T): VisitBritain/Britain On View/GettyImages; p. 64 (B): GM Visuals/Blend Images/GettyImages; p. 65 (Ex 6.1): T.T./Taxi/GettyImages; p. 65 (Ex 6.2): Jade/Blend Images/GettyImages; p. 65 (Ex 6.3): Hero Images/Hero Images/GettyImages; p. 65 (Ex 6.4): Todor Tsvetkov/E+/GettyImages; p. 65 (Ex 6.5): Hero Images/Hero Images/GettyImages; p. 65 (Ex 6.6): Lucia Lambriex/Taxi/GettyImages; p. 65 (Ex 6.7): Er Creatives Services Ltd/Iconica/GettyImages; p. 65 (Ex 6.8): Susan Chiang/E+/GettyImages; p. 65 (Ex 6.9): PhotoAlto/Teo Lannie/PhotoAlto Agency RF Collections/GettyImages; p. 66 (TL): Maximilian Stock Ltd/Photolibrary/GettyImages; p. 66 (TR): Grafner/iStock/Getty Images Plus/GettyImages; p. 66 (CL): Freek Gout/EyeEm/EyeEm/GettyImages; p. 66 (CR): Vstock LLC/GettyImages; p. 66 (BL): mashabuba/E+/GettyImages; p. 66 (BR): Tom Merton/Caiaimage/GettyImages; p. 70: Nicolas McComber/iStock/Getty Images Plus/GettyImages; p. 73 (bank): Keith Brofsky/Photodisc/GettyImages; p. 73 (coffee shop): Jake Curtis/Iconica/GettyImages; p. 73 (petrol pump): David Lees/Taxi/GettyImages; p. 73 (book store): Jetta Productions/The Image Bank/GettyImages; p. 73 (clothing store): Blend Images - Erik Isakson/Brand X Pictures/GettyImages; p. 73 (post office): Matt Cardy/Stringer/Getty Images Europe/GettyImages; p. 73 (supermarket): Johner Images/GettyImages; p. 73 (pharmacy): Caiaimage/Rafal Rodzoch/Caiaimage/GettyImages; p. 76: Leonardo Patrizi/E+/GettyImages; p. 79 (Ex 1.1): Y.Nakajima/un/ANYONE/amana images/GettyImages; p. 79 (Ex 1.2): John Lund/Marc Romanelli/Blend Images/GettyImages; p. 79 (Ex 1.3): Maskot/Maskot/GettyImages; p. 79 (Ex 1.4): UniversalImagesGroup/Universal Images Group/GettyImages; p. 79 (Ex 1.5): ullstein bild/ullstein bild/GettyImages; p. 79 (Ex 1.6): Geography Photos/Universal Images Group/GettyImages; p. 79 (Ex 1.7): CommerceandCultureAgency/The Image Bank/GettyImages; p. 79 (Ex 1.8): Jose Luis Pelaez Inc/Blend Images/GettyImages; p. 80 (Alisha): Dougal Waters/DigitalVision/GettyImages; p. 80 (Kim): Hero Images/Hero Images/GettyImages; p. 82: ullstein bild/ullstein bild/GettyImages; p. 83: Tetra Images - Chris Hackett/Brand X Pictures/GettyImages; p. 85: Westend61/GettyImages; p. 86 (T): Walter Bibikow/AWL Images/GettyImages; p. 86 (C): Michele Falzone/Photolibrary/GettyImages; p. 86 (B): Takashi Yagihashi/amana images/GettyImages; p. 87 (Ex 3.1): Photos.com/PHOTOS.com>>/Getty Images Plus/GettyImages; p. 87 (Ex 3.2): Piero Pomponi/Hulton Archive/GettyImages; p. 87 (Ex 3.3): KMazur/WireImage/GettyImages; p. 87 (Ex 3.4): Nancy R. Schiff/Hulton Archive/GettyImages; p. 87 (Ex 3.5): API/Gamma-Rapho/GettyImages; p. 87 (Ex 3.6): Jack Mitchell/Archive Photos/GettyImages; p. 88: Christopher Futcher/E+/GettyImages; p. 89: Mel Melcon/Los Angeles Times/GettyImages; p. 90 (T): Kevin Dodge/Blend Images/GettyImages; p. 90 (B): Thomas Barwick/Taxi/GettyImages; p. 91 (L): Stockbyte/Stockbyte/GettyImages; p. 91 (R): nyul/iStock/Getty Images Plus/GettyImages; p. 93: freemixer/iStock/Getty Images Plus/GettyImages; p. 94: Echo/Cultura/GettyImages; p. 95: Stockbyte/Stockbyte/GettyImages; p. 96 (T): Thanks for viewing! www.johnsteelephoto.com/Moment/GettyImages; p. 96 (B): Giordano Cipriani/The Image Bank/GettyImages.

1 What's your name?

1 Complete the conversations. Use the names in the box.

☐ John   ☐ Mr. Garcia   ☐ Ms. Baker   ☑ Nancy

Hi, __Nancy__.

Hello, _____.

It's nice to meet you, _____.

Nice to meet you, too, _____.

2 Complete the conversations. Use *my*, *your*, *his*, or *her*.

1. **A:** Hi. What's ____your____ name?
   B: _____ name is Lisa. And what's _____ name?
   A: _____ name is James.

2. **A:** What's _____ name?
   B: _____ name is Michael.
   A: And what's _____ name?
   B: _____ name is Susan.

3 Complete the conversations.

1. **A:** Hello, _____Mr._____ Wilson.
   B: _____ morning, David. _____ are you?
   A: _____ OK, thank you.

2. **A:** Hi. How are _____, Mrs. Turner?
   B: I'm just _____, thank you. How about _____, _____ Smith?
   A: Pretty _____, thanks.

3. **A:** How's it _____, Ken?
   B: Great. _____ are you doing?
   A: Pretty good.

4 Choose the correct responses.

1. **A:** Hi, Tony.
   B: _____Hello._____
   - Hello.
   - It's nice to meet you.

2. **A:** My name is Ellen Miller.
   B: _____
   - It's Williams.
   - I'm Rob Williams.

3. **A:** Hello, Carol. How's it going?
   B: _____
   - Fine, thanks.
   - Nice to meet you, too.

4. **A:** How do you spell your last name?
   B: _____
   - R-O-G-E-R-S.
   - It's Rogers.

5. **A:** I'm Rich Martinez.
   B: _____
   - Nice to meet you, too.
   - It's nice to meet you.

5 Spell the numbers.

1. 2 _____two_____
2. 3 _____
3. 8 _____
4. 1 _____
5. 7 _____
6. 10 _____

7. 5 _____
8. 6 _____
9. 0 _____
10. 9 _____
11. 4 _____

What's your name?

6 Write the telephone numbers and email addresses.

1. two-one-two, five-five-five, six-one-one-five   212-555-6115
2. A-M-Y dash L-O-P-E-Z eight-two at C-U-P dot O-R-G   amy-lopez82@cup.org
3. six-oh-four, five-five-five, four-seven-three-one
4. nine-four-nine, five-five-five, three-eight-oh-two
5. B-R-I-A-N dot J-O-H-N-S-O-N zero-three-nine at C-U-P dot O-R-G
6. seven-seven-three, five-five-five, one-seven-seven-nine
7. M-A-R-I-A-B-R-A-D-Y underscore seven at C-U-P dot O-R-G
8. T-I-N-A dash F-O-X underscore nine-five-two at C-U-P dot O-R-G

7 Complete the conversations. Write 'm, 're, or 's.

1. **A:** What 's your name?
   B: I _____ Momoko Sato.
   A: It _____ nice to meet you, Momoko.

2. **A:** Hello. I _____ Josh Brown. I _____ in your English class.
   B: Yes, and you _____ in my math class, too.

3. **A:** What _____ his name?
   B: It _____ Chris Allen.
   A: He _____ in our English class.
   B: You _____ right!

Unit 1

8 Complete the conversations. Use the words in the box.

☐ am ☐ he's ☐ I'm not ☐ it's ☐ you
☐ are ☐ I'm ☐ is ✓ me ☐ you're

1. **Amy:** Excuse _____me_____ . Are _____ Alex Walker?

   Carlos: No, _____ . _____ over there.

   Amy: Oh, _____ sorry.

2. **Amy:** Excuse me. _____ you Alex Walker?

   Alex: Yes, I _____ .

   Amy: Hi, Alex. My name _____ Amy Clark.

   Alex: Oh, _____ in my English class.

   Amy: That's right. _____ nice to meet you.

   Alex: Nice to meet you, too.

9 Complete the conversation. Use the questions in the box.

☐ What's your name?
☐ And how do you spell your last name?
✓ Are you Andrea Nelson?
☐ And what's your email address?
☐ What's your phone number?
☐ How do you spell your first name?

A: Hi. <u>Are you Andrea Nelson?</u>

B: No, I'm not.

A: Oh, I'm sorry. _____

B: Kerry Moore.

A: _____

B: K-E-R-R-Y.

A: _____

B: M-O-O-R-E.

A: _____

B: It's 618-555-7120.

A: _____

B: It's kmoore19@cup.org.

What's your name? **5**

10 Hello and good-bye!

A Complete the conversations. Use the words in parentheses.

1. **A:** _Hi._
   (Hi. / Excuse me.) How are you?
   B: I'm fine, thanks.

2. **A:** _____
   (Hello. / Good-bye.)
   B: See you tomorrow.

3. **A:** _____
   (Excuse me. / Thank you.) Are you Min-ji Park?
   B: Yes, I am. It's nice to meet you.

4. **A:** _____
   (Good evening. / Good night.)
   B: Hello.

B Match the pictures with the conversations in part A.

a. _1_

b. _____

c. _____

d. _____

2 Where are my keys?

1 What are these things?

A What's in the picture? Write the things.

1. a backpack
2. _____
3. _____
4. _____
5. _____
6. _____
7. _____
8. _____

B What's in the picture? Write sentences.

1. This is a backpack.
2. _____
3. _____
4. _____
5. _____
6. _____
7. _____
8. _____

2 Complete the chart with the words in the box.

- ✓ doors
- ☐ purses
- ☐ desks
- ☐ energy bars
- ✓ books
- ☐ umbrellas
- ☐ hairbrushes
- ☐ tablets
- ✓ quizzes
- ☐ laptops
- ☐ keys
- ☐ boxes

/z/	/s/	/ɪz/
doors	books	quizzes

3 Complete the questions with *this* or *these*. Then answer the questions.

1. **A:** What's _____this_____ ?
   B: It's a cell phone.

2. **A:** What's _____ ?
   B: _____

3. **A:** What are _____ ?
   B: _____

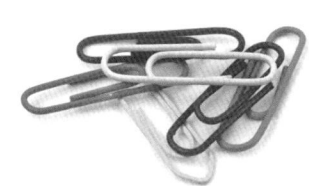

4. **A:** What are _____ ?
   B: _____

5. **A:** What are _____ ?
   B: _____

6. **A:** What's _____ ?
   B: _____

4 Complete the conversation. Use the words in the box.

☐ a   ☐ 's   ☐ this   ☐ they   ☐ you
☐ an   ✓ it's   ☐ these   ☐ they're ☐ you're

Clara: Wow! What's this?

Kevin: _____It's_____ a purse.

Clara: Oh, cool. Thank _____ , Kevin.

Kevin: _____ welcome.

Eva: Now open _____ box.

Clara: OK. What _____ this?

Eva: It's _____ tablet case.

Clara: Oh, thank you, Eva. And what are _____ ?

Eva: _____ 're sunglasses.

Clara: Thanks! _____ great!

Laura: Open this, too!

Clara: Oh, it's _____ umbrella. Thanks, Laura!

Unit 2

5 Complete the conversations. Use the answers in the box.

☐ Yes, I am.   ☐ Yes, it is.   ☐ Yes, they are.   ☐ It's
☐ No, I'm not.   ☐ No, it's not.   ✓ No, they're not.   ☐ They're

1. **A:** Are these your books?
   B: _No, they're not._ My books are in my bag.

2. **A:** Excuse me. Is this the math class?
   B: _____ And I'm your teacher.

3. **A:** Is my purse on the chair?
   B: _____ It's under the table.

4. **A:** Where's my laptop?
   B: _____ in your backpack.

5. **A:** Where are your glasses?
   B: _____ in my purse.

6. **A:** Hi. Are you in my math class?
   B: _____ And I'm in your English class, too!

7. **A:** Are these your keys?
   B: _____ Thank you.

8. **A:** Excuse me. Are you Min-soo Cho?
   B: _____ My name is Jin-ho Han. Min-soo isn't in this class.

Where are my keys? 9

6 Complete the conversations.

1. **A:** Oh no! Where ___is___ my tablet?
   B: Is _____ in your backpack?
   A: No, it's _____ .
   B: Hmm. _____ it under your math book?
   A: Yes, it is! Thank you!

2. **A:** _____ this my cell phone?
   B: No, _____ not. It's my cell phone.
   A: Sorry. _____ is my cell phone?
   B: Is _____ in your purse?
   A: Oh, yes, it _____ . Thanks.

3. **A:** Where _____ my keys?
   B: Are _____ in your pocket?
   A: No, they're _____ .
   B: _____ they on the table?
   A: Hmm. Yes, _____ are. Thanks.

4. **A:** _____ my notebook in your backpack?
   B: No, _____ not. Sorry.
   A: Hmm. _____ is my notebook?
   B: _____ it behind your laptop?
   A: Let me see. Yes, it _____ . Thank you!

7 Answer the questions. Use your own information.

1. Are you a teacher?
   No, I'm not. I'm a student.
2. Is your name Akiko Nakayama?
   _____
3. Is your workbook on your desk?
   _____
4. Is your phone number 806-555-0219?
   _____
5. Are you in a math class?
   _____

8 Complete the sentences. Use the prepositions in the box.

☐ behind ☑ in ☐ in front of ☐ next to ☐ on ☐ under

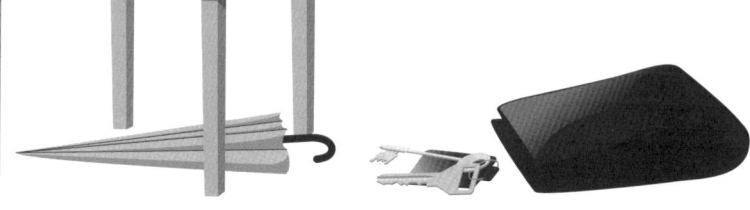

1. The notebook is ___in___ the backpack.
2. The umbrella is _____ the table. 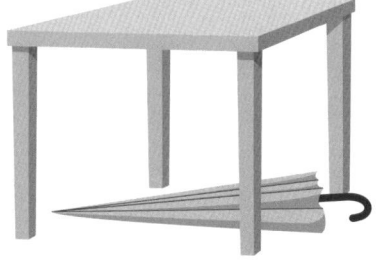
3. The keys are _____ the wallet.
4. The pen is _____ the purse. 
5. The laptop is _____ the desk. 
6. The wastebasket is _____ the chair. 

Where are my keys? 11

9 Where are these things?

A Look at the picture. Write questions and answers about the things in parentheses.

1. **A:** <u>Where is the backpack?</u> (backpack)
   B: <u>It's next to the table.</u>
2. **A:** _____ (books)
   B: _____
3. **A:** _____ (cell phone)
   B: _____
4. **A:** _____ (pens)
   B: _____
5. **A:** _____ (purse)
   B: _____
6. **A:** _____ (sunglasses)
   B: _____

B Write two more questions and answers about the picture.

1. **A:** _____
   B: _____
2. **A:** _____
   B: _____

3 Where are you from?

1 Cities and countries

A Complete the chart with the languages and nationalities in the box.

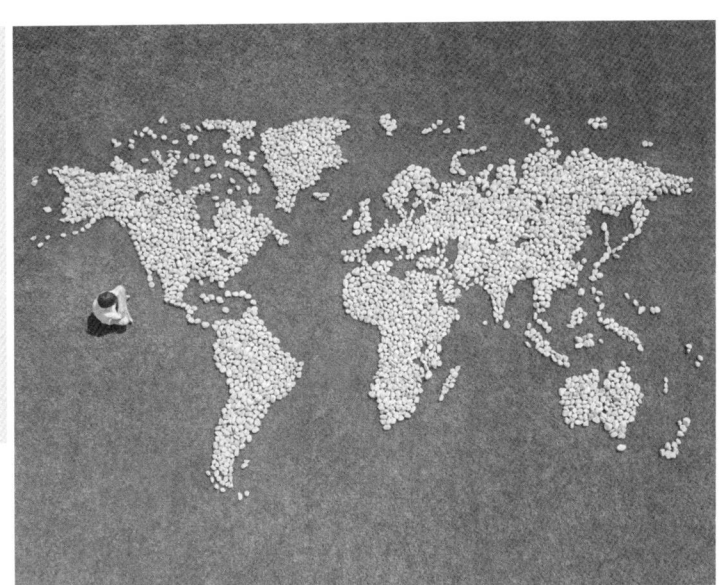

- ☐ Arabic
- ☐ Argentine
- ☑ Brazilian
- ☐ Canadian
- ☐ Colombian
- ☐ Egyptian
- ☐ English
- ☐ French
- ☐ Japanese
- ☐ Japanese
- ☐ Korean
- ☑ Portuguese
- ☐ South Korean
- ☐ Spanish
- ☐ Spanish
- ☐ Turkish
- ☐ Turkish

Countries	Nationalities	Languages
Brazil	Brazilian	Portuguese
Colombia		
South Korea		
Canada		
Turkey		
Argentina		
Japan		
Egypt		

B Where are these cities? Complete the sentences with the countries in part A.

1. Istanbul and Ankara _are in Turkey._
2. Bogotá _____
3. Tokyo _____
4. São Paulo and Rio de Janeiro _____
5. Seoul and Daejeon _____
6. Buenos Aires _____
7. Vancouver and Ottawa _____
8. Cairo _____

2 Complete the conversations with am, 'm, are, 're, is, or 's.

1. **A:** _____Are_____ you and your family from New Zealand?
   B: No, we _____ not. We _____ from Australia.
   A: Oh, so you _____ Australian.
   B: Yes, I _____ . I _____ from Melbourne.

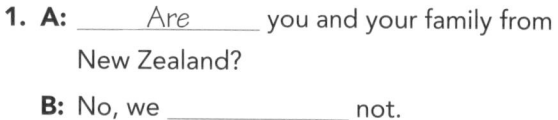

2. **A:** _____ Brazil in Central America?
   B: No, it _____ not. It _____ in South America.
   A: Oh. _____ we from Brazil, Dad?
   B: Yes, we _____ . We _____ from Brazil originally, but we _____ here in the U.S. now.

3. **A:** _____ this your wallet?
   B: Yes, it _____ . Thanks.
   A: And _____ these your sunglasses?
   B: Yes, they _____ .
   A: Well, they _____ very nice sunglasses.
   B: Thank you!

4. **A:** _____ your English teacher from the U.S.?
   B: No, she _____ not. She _____ from Canada. Montreal, Canada.
   A: _____ English her first language?
   B: No, it _____ not. Her first language _____ French.

3 Answer the questions.

1. **A:** Are they from Colombia?
   B: No, they're not. They're from Brazil.

2. **A:** Is she from India?
   B: _____

3. **A:** Is she from Canada?
   B: _____

4. **A:** Are they in Mexico?
   B: _____

5. **A:** Is he in Bangkok?
   B: _____

6. **A:** Are they in Egypt?
   B: _____

Where are you from?

4 Spell the numbers.

1. 14 _____fourteen_____
2. 40 _____
3. 60 _____
4. 13 _____
5. 27 _____
6. 102 _____
7. 11 _____
8. 30 _____
9. 18 _____
10. 80 _____

5 Complete the conversations with the correct responses.

1. **A:** Where are they from?
   B: _She's from the U.K., and he's from the U.S._
   - She's Emily Blunt, and he's John Krasinski.
   - She's from the U.K., and he's from the U.S.

2. **A:** Is your first language English?
   B: _____
   - No, it's Japan.
   - No, it's Japanese.

3. **A:** What are they like?
   B: _____
   - They're very serious.
   - They're in Hong Kong.

4. **A:** Who's that?
   B: _____
   - He's the new math teacher.
   - It's my new tablet.

5. **A:** Where are Rahul and his family?
   B: _____
   - They're in the U.S. now.
   - They're from Mumbai.

6. **A:** How old is he now?
   B: _____
   - It's twenty-eight.
   - He's twenty-eight.

7. **A:** What's Marrakech like?
   B: _____
   - It's in Morocco.
   - It's very interesting.

Unit 3

6 Descriptions

A Write sentences about the people in the pictures. Use the words in the box.

- ☐ funny   ☐ serious   ☐ talkative
- ☐ heavy   ☐ short   ☐ tall
- ☐ kind   ☑ shy   ☐ thin

1. Julia is _____shy_____ .

2. Mark and Carlos are _____ .

3. Brian is _____ and Owen is _____ .

4. Daniel is _____ .

5. Mariko is _____ and Ben is _____ .

6. Ginny is _____ .

7. Dr. Lopez is _____ .

B Answer the questions.

1. Is Ben tall? _Yes, he is._
2. Is Ginny serious? _____
3. Is Owen thin? _____
4. Is Julia young? _____
5. Are Mark and Carlos male? _____
6. Is Dr. Lopez old? _____
7. Are you kind? _____
8. Are you shy? _____

Where are you from?

7 Complete the conversations. Use the words in the boxes.

☐ her   ☐ not   ☑ what's
☐ is   ☐ she's ☐ where

1. **A:** Annette, ____what's____ your best friend like?
   B: _____ very nice. _____ name is Valentina. I call her Tina.
   A: _____ is she from? _____ she from Spain?
   B: No, she's _____ . She's from Italy.

☐ are   ☐ my   ☐ we're
☐ her   ☐ we   ☐ what's

2. **A:** Toshi, are you and Naomi from Japan?
   B: Yes, _____ are. _____ from Osaka.
   A: _____ your first language?
   B: _____ first language is Japanese, but Naomi's first language is English. _____ parents _____ from New York originally.

8 Answer the questions. Use your own information.

1. Where are you from?
   _____

2. What's your first language?
   _____

3. How are you today?
   _____

4. Where is your teacher from?
   _____

5. What is your teacher like?
   _____

6. What are you like?
   _____

4 Is this coat yours?

1 Label the clothes. Use the words in the box.

- [ ] belt
- [ ] high heels
- [ ] skirt
- [ ] T-shirt
- [ ] blouse
- [✓] jacket
- [ ] sneakers
- [ ] cap
- [ ] shorts
- [ ] socks

1. _jacket_
2. _____
3. _____
4. _____
5. _____
6. _____
7. _____
8. _____
9. _____
10. _____

2 What clothes don't belong? Check (✓) the things.

For work	For home	For cold weather	For warm weather
☐ shirt	☐ T-shirt	☐ boots	☐ swimsuit
✓ shorts	☐ shorts	☐ scarf	☐ T-shirt
☐ tie	☐ suit	☐ shorts	☐ boots
☐ belt	☐ dress	☐ pants	☐ sneakers
✓ swimsuit	☐ jeans	☐ sweater	☐ shorts
☐ shoes	☐ pajamas	☐ gloves	☐ sweater
☐ jacket	☐ coat	☐ T-shirt	☐ cap

3 What things in your classroom are these colors? Write sentences.

beige   brown   gray   light blue   pink   red   yellow
black   dark blue   green   orange   purple   white

1. My desk is brown. (brown)
2. Celia's bag is purple. (purple)
3. _____ (gray)
4. _____ (white)
5. _____ (red)
6. _____ (green)
7. _____ (black)
8. _____
9. _____
10. _____

4 Whose clothes are these?

Max    Maya    Lisa

A Complete the conversations.

1. **A:** Whose _scarf is this_ ?
   B: _It's Maya's_ .

2. **A:** Whose _____ ?
   B: _____ .

3. **A:** Whose _____ ?
   B: _____ .

4. **A:** Whose _____ ?
   B: _____ .

5. **A:** Whose _____ ?
   B: _____ .

6. **A:** Whose _____ ?
   B: _____ .

B Complete the conversations with the correct words in parentheses.

1. **A:** ___Whose___ (Whose / His) T-shirt is this? Is it Ayumi's?
   B: No, it's not _____ (her / hers). It's _____ (my / mine).

2. **A:** Are these _____ (your / yours) jeans?
   B: No, they aren't _____ (my / mine) jeans. Let's ask Mohammed. I think they're _____ (his / he's).

3. **A:** Are these Stephanie's and Jennifer's socks?
   B: No, they aren't _____ (their / theirs). They're _____ (your / yours).
   A: I don't think so. These socks are white, and _____ (my / mine) are blue.

Is this coat yours? **21**

5 What season is it? How is the weather? Write two sentences about each picture.

1. It's fall.
   It's very windy.

2. _____
   _____

3. _____
   _____

4. _____
   _____

5. _____
   _____

6. _____
   _____

Unit 4

6 Waiting for the bus

A Write sentences. Use the words in parentheses.

1. Pablo is wearing a tie. (tie)
2. Steven and Carolina are wearing boots. (boots)
3. _____ (T-shirt)
4. _____ (skirt)
5. _____ (dress)
6. _____ (sneakers)
7. _____ (scarf)
8. _____ (hats)

B Correct the false sentences.

1. Sung-min is wearing jeans.
   No, he isn't. / No, he's not. He's wearing shorts.

2. Liz and Pablo are wearing raincoats.
   _____

3. Carolina is wearing a skirt.
   _____

4. Allison is wearing pajamas.
   _____

5. Carolina and Liz are wearing T-shirts.
   _____

6. Steven and Pablo are wearing shorts.
   _____

Is this coat yours?

7 Complete the sentences.

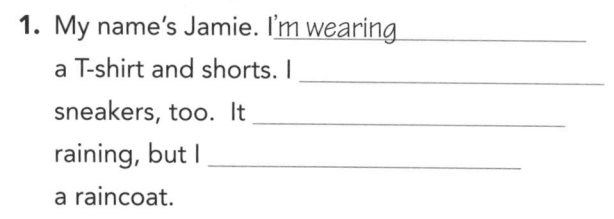

1. My name's Jamie. I'm wearing a T-shirt and shorts. I _____ sneakers, too. It _____ raining, but I _____ a raincoat.

2. It's winter, so Maria _____ high heels – she _____ boots. She _____ a scarf, but she _____ a hat.

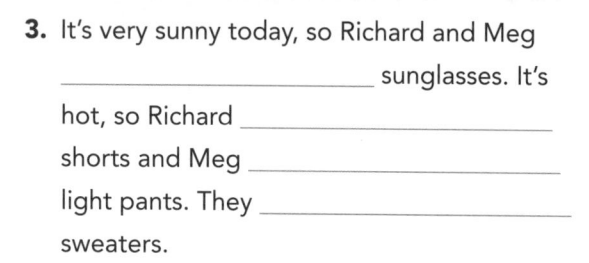

3. It's very sunny today, so Richard and Meg _____ sunglasses. It's hot, so Richard _____ shorts and Meg _____ light pants. They _____ sweaters.

4. Ed _____ a suit. He _____ a scarf, but he _____ a tie. He _____ shoes and socks. It's very windy.

8 Complete these sentences with *and*, *but*, or *so*.

1. He's wearing jeans and sneakers, _____and_____ he's wearing a T-shirt.
2. It's very cold outside, _____ I'm not wearing a coat.
3. Her skirt is blue, _____ her blouse is blue, too.
4. It's raining, _____ I need an umbrella.
5. He's wearing an expensive suit, _____ he's wearing sneakers.
6. It's summer and it's very sunny, _____ it's hot.

5 What time is it?

1 Write each sentence a different way.

1. It's midnight.   It's twelve o'clock at night.
2. It's 7:00 A.M.   _____
3. It's 2:45 P.M.   _____
4. It's 9:20 A.M.   _____
5. It's 6:15 P.M.   _____
6. It's 11:00 P.M.   _____
7. It's 3:30 A.M.   _____
8. It's 12:00 P.M.   _____

2 What time is it in each city? Write the time in two different ways.

1. It's 10:00 A.M. in Seattle.
   It's ten o'clock in the morning.
2. _____
3. _____
4. _____
5. _____
6. _____

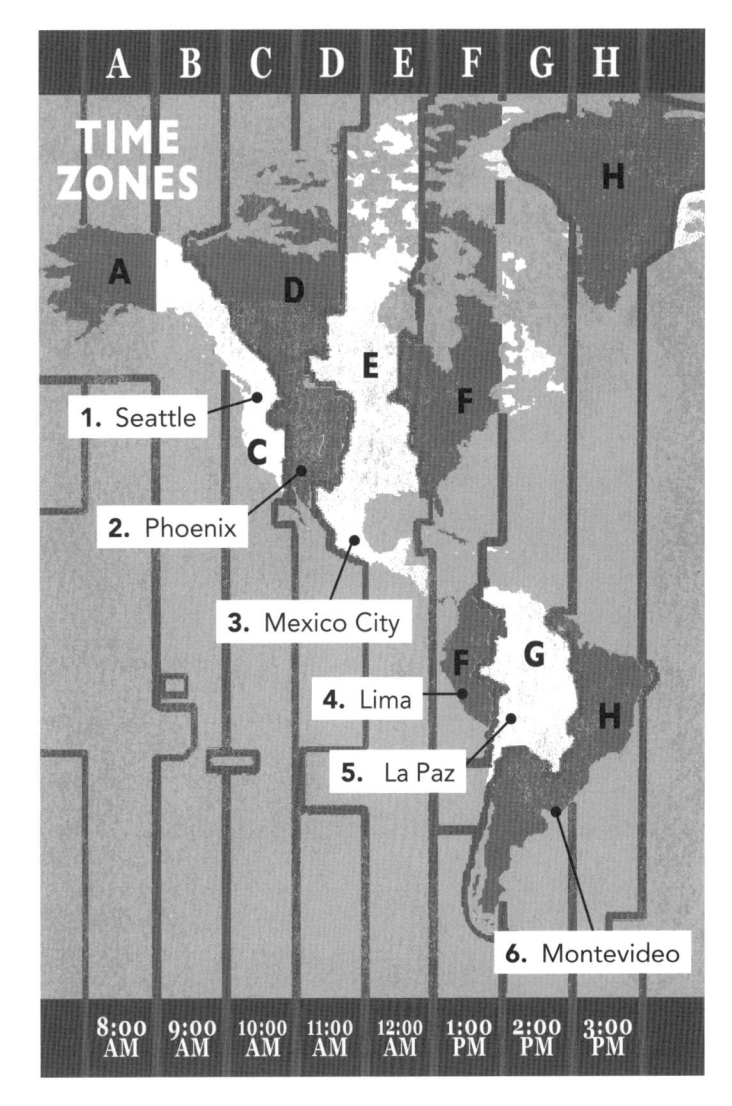

3 What time is it? Use the sentences in the box.

- ✓ It's a quarter after five.
- ☐ It's a quarter to two.
- ☐ It's four-thirty.
- ☐ It's nine-oh-three.
- ☐ It's ten after eight.
- ☐ It's twelve o'clock.

1. It's a quarter after five.
2. _____
3. _____
4. _____
5. _____
6. _____

4 Complete the sentences. Write each time a different way.

1. It's six in the morning. It's six ____A.M.____
2. It's 10:00 P.M. It's ten at _____ .
3. It's 5:15. It's five- _____ .
4. It's 7:00 P.M. It's seven in the _____ .
5. It's 4:30. It's four- _____ .
6. It's 8:00 A.M. It's eight in the _____ .
7. It's twelve P.M. It's _____ .
8. It's 2:00 P.M. It's two in the _____ .
9. It's twelve A.M. It's _____ .
10. It's 6:45. It's a _____ to seven.
11. It's 11:15. It's a quarter _____ eleven.

Unit 5

5 What are these people doing? Write sentences. Use the words in the box.

☐ call a friend   ☑ make coffee   ☐ take a walk
☐ drive   ☐ ride a bike   ☐ watch a movie
☐ have breakfast ☐ shop   ☐ work

1. _He's making coffee._
2. _____ 
3. _____ 
4. _____ 
5. _____ 
6. _____ 
7. _____ 
8. _____ 
9. _____ 

What time is it? 27

6 Answer these questions.

1. Is Salma sleeping?
   <u>No, she's not. She's studying.</u>

2. Are Richard and Laura playing tennis?
   <u>No, they're not. They're dancing.</u>

3. Is Charles visiting friends?
   _____

4. Is Jerry eating dinner?
   _____

5. Are Mary and Jennifer checking their messages?
   _____

6. Is Carol listening to music?
   _____

7. Is Kevin driving?
   _____

8. Are the friends watching a movie?
   _____

Unit 5

7 Write questions about these people. Use the words in parentheses. Then answer the questions.

1. **A:** Is Min wearing jeans?
   (Min / wear jeans)
   B: No, she's not. She's wearing a dress.
2. **A:** _____
   (Bob / drink soda)
   B: _____
3. **A:** _____
   (Jason and Beth / watch a movie)
   B: _____
4. **A:** _____
   (Adriana / wear jeans)
   B: _____
5. **A:** _____
   (Amy and Gabriela / chat online)
   B: _____
6. **A:** _____
   (Daniel / talk to Adriana)
   B: _____
7. **A:** _____
   (Bob / wear shorts)
   B: _____
8. **A:** _____
   (Min / talk on the phone)
   B: _____

What time is it? 29

8 Write questions and answers. Use *What + doing* and the words in parentheses.

1. **A:** What is Linda doing? (Linda)
   B: She's checking her messages. (check her messages)
2. **A:** What are you and Akira doing? (you and Akira)
   B: We're eating lunch. (eat lunch)
3. **A:** _____ (Tom and Donna)
   B: _____ (visit friends)
4. **A:** _____ (Sandra)
   B: _____ (get up)
5. **A:** _____ (you and Isabella)
   B: _____ (ride bikes)
6. **A:** _____ (Diego and Patricia)
   B: _____ (work)
7. **A:** _____ (Tim)
   B: _____ (listen to music)
8. **A:** _____ (you)
   B: _____ (study English)
9. **A:** _____ (Sonya and Annie)
   B: _____ (have dinner)
10. **A:** _____ (I)
    B: _____ (finish this exercise)

9 What are you doing? What are your friends doing? Write sentences.

1. _____
2. _____
3. _____
4. _____
5. _____
6. _____

Unit 5

6 I ride my bike to school.

1 Family

A Angela is talking about her family. Complete the sentences with the words in the box.

- [ ] brother
- [ ] father
- [✓] parents
- [ ] wife
- [ ] children
- [ ] husband
- [ ] sister
- [ ] daughters
- [ ] mother
- [ ] son

Family Photos   Home   Gallery   Log in

Larry   Alice   Nick   Angela

Avery   Ethan   Bella

1. Alice and Larry are my __parents__ . Alice is my _____ , and Larry is my _____ .
2. Nick is my _____ . I'm his _____ .
3. Ethan, Avery, and Bella are our _____ . Avery and Bella are our _____ , and Ethan is our _____ . Avery is Bella's _____ , and Ethan is her _____ .

B Write four sentences about your family.

1. _____
2. _____
3. _____
4. _____

2 Complete the conversation with the correct words in parentheses.

Christine: So, do you live downtown, Sarah?
Sarah: Yes, I ____live____ with my brother.
(live / lives)
He _____ an apartment near here.
(have / has)
Christine: Oh, so you _____ to work.
(walk / walks)
Sarah: Actually, I _____ walk to work in
(don't / doesn't)
the morning. I _____ the bus to work,
(take / takes)
and then I _____ home at night.
(walk / walks)
What about you?
Christine: Well, my husband and I _____ a house
(have / has)
in the suburbs now, so I _____ to work.
(drive / drives)
My husband doesn't _____ downtown.
(work / works)
He _____ in the suburbs near our house,
(work / works)
so he _____ to work by bus.
(go / goes)

3 Third-person singular –s endings

A Write the third-person singular forms of these verbs.

1. dance ____dances____
2. do ____does____
3. go _____
4. have _____
5. live _____
6. ride _____
7. sleep _____
8. study _____
9. take _____
10. use _____
11. walk _____
12. watch _____

B Practice the words in part A. Then add them to the chart.

s = /s/	s = /z/	(e)s = /ɪz/	irregular
_____	_____	____dances____	____does____
_____	_____	_____	_____
_____	_____	_____	_____

4 True or false?

A Are these sentences true for you? Check (✓) True or False.

	True	False
1. I ride the bus to school.	☐	☐
2. I have a car.	☐	☐
3. I live in the suburbs.	☐	☐
4. I have brothers / a brother.	☐	☐
5. I do my homework at the library.	☐	☐
6. I do my homework alone.	☐	☐
7. I live in a house.	☐	☐
8. I have sisters / a sister.	☐	☐
9. I live with my parents.	☐	☐
10. I work in an office.	☐	☐

B Correct the false statements in part A.

<u>I don't ride the bus to school. I ride my bike to school.</u>

_____
_____
_____
_____
_____
_____
_____
_____
_____
_____
_____

I ride my bike to school.

5 Write about Daniela's weekly schedule. Use the words in parentheses.

	Monday	Tuesday	Wednesday	Thursday	Friday
7:00 A.M.	get up ──►
8:00 A.M.	go to work ───►
9:00 A.M.					
10:00 A.M.					
11:00 A.M.	have lunch ───►
12:00 P.M.					
1:00 P.M.					
2:00 P.M.	take a walk ──►
3:00 P.M.					
4:00 P.M.					
5:00 P.M.	finish work ──►
6:00 P.M.	play basketball	go to class	eat dinner with my family	go to class	watch a movie

1. <u>She gets up at 7:00 every day.</u> (7:00)
2. _____ (8:00)
3. _____ (11:00)
4. _____ (2:00)
5. _____ (5:00)
6. _____ (6:00 / Mondays)
7. _____ (6:00 / Tuesdays and Thursdays)
8. _____ (6:00 / Fridays)

6 Write something you do and something you don't do on each day. Use the phrases in the box or your own information.

check email	exercise	have dinner late	sleep late
drive a car	get up early	play video games	talk on the phone
eat breakfast	go to school	see my friends	watch a movie

1. Monday <u>I get up early on Mondays. I don't sleep late on Mondays.</u>
2. Tuesday _____
3. Wednesday _____
4. Thursday _____
5. Friday _____
6. Saturday _____
7. Sunday _____

7 Complete these conversations with *at*, *in*, or *on*. (If you don't need a preposition, write Ø.)

1. **A:** Do you go to bed __Ø__ late __on__ weekends?
   B: Yes, I do. I go to bed _____ midnight. But I go to bed _____ early _____ weekdays.

2. **A:** Do you study _____ the afternoon?
   B: No, I study _____ the morning _____ weekends, and I study _____ the evening _____ Mondays and Wednesdays.

3. **A:** What time do you get up _____ the morning _____ weekdays?
   B: I get up _____ 6:00 _____ every day.

4. **A:** Do you have English class _____ the morning?
   B: No, I have English _____ 3:30 _____ the afternoon _____ Tuesdays and Thursdays. _____ Mondays, Wednesdays, and Fridays, our class is _____ 5:00.

8 Write questions to complete the conversations.

1. **A:** Do you live alone?
   B: No, I don't live alone. I live with my mom and dad.

2. **A:** _____
   B: Yes, my family and I watch television in the afternoon.

3. **A:** _____
   B: Yes, I get up early on Fridays.
   A: _____
   B: I get up at 5:30.

4. **A:** _____
   B: No, my sister doesn't drive to work.
   A: _____
   B: No, she doesn't take the bus. She takes the train.

5. **A:** _____
   B: No, my dad doesn't work on weekends.
   A: _____
   B: He works on weekdays.

6. **A:** _____
   B: Yes, my mom works in the city. She's a restaurant manager.
   A: _____
   B: No, she doesn't use public transportation. She drives to work.

7. **A:** _____
   B: Yes, we have a big lunch on Sundays.
   A: _____
   B: We have lunch at 1:00.

9 Write each sentence a different way. Use the sentences in the box.

- ☐ He goes to work before noon.
- ☐ I don't work far from here.
- ☑ Kimberly is Dan's wife.
- ☐ She doesn't get up early on Sundays.
- ☐ We don't live in the suburbs.
- ☐ We take the bus, the train, or the subway.

1. Dan is Kimberly's husband.
   <u>Kimberly is Dan's wife.</u>

2. We have an apartment in the city.

3. We use public transportation.

4. He goes to work in the morning.

5. My office is near here.

6. She sleeps late on Sundays.

10 Answer the questions about your schedule.

1. What do you do on weekdays?

2. What do you do on weekends?

3. What do you do on Friday nights?

4. What do you do on Sunday mornings?

7 Does it have a view?

1 Label the parts of the house.

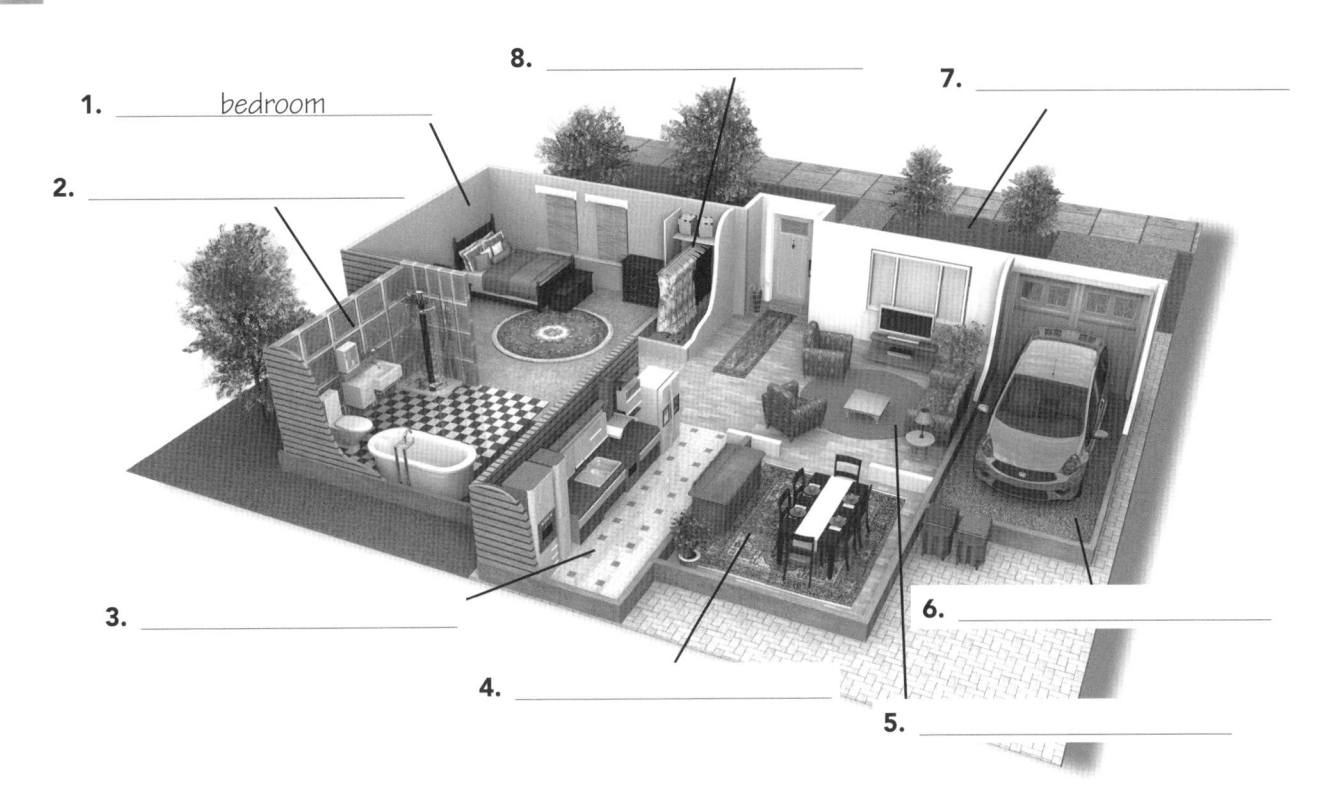

1. _____bedroom_____
2. _____
3. _____
4. _____
5. _____
6. _____
7. _____
8. _____

2 Complete the conversation. Use the sentences in the box.

☐ No, I don't. I live with my sisters.   ☐ Yes, it has three bedrooms.
☑ No, I live in an apartment.   ☐ Yes, it has a great view of the city.

Ji-hye: Do you live in a house, Fernanda?

Fernanda: No, I live in an apartment.

Ji-hye: Well, is it very big?

Fernanda: _____

Ji-hye: Does it have a view?

Fernanda: _____

Ji-hye: Oh, that's great! And do you live alone?

Fernanda: _____

3 Complete the conversation with the correct words in parentheses.

Al: ____Do____ you _____ near here, Brandon?
      (Do / Does)   (live / lives)

Brandon: Yes, I _____ . My wife and I _____ on Main Street.
             (do / does)   (live / lives)

Al: Oh, do you _____ in an apartment?
                   (live / lives)

Brandon: No, we _____ . We _____ a house.
             (don't / doesn't)   (have / has)

Al: Oh, great! _____ you _____ children?
                  (Do / Does)   (have / has)

Brandon: No, we _____ .
             (don't / doesn't)

But my mother _____ with us.
              (live / lives)

Al: Really? Does she do a lot of work at home?

Brandon: Yes, she _____ .
             (do / does)

In fact, she _____ dinner every night!
             (cook / cooks)

Al: You're lucky! I _____ alone,
                       (live / lives)

and I _____ my own dinner.
      (cook / cooks)

4 Answer these questions with your information. Use short answers.

1. Do you live in a house? _Yes, I do. / No, I don't._
2. Do you have a garage? _____
3. Do you live with your family? _____
4. Does your city or town have a park? _____
5. Does your teacher have a car? _____
6. Do you and your classmates speak English? _____
7. Do you and your classmates study together? _____
8. Does your classroom have a view? _____
9. Does your school have a lobby? _____
10. Does your city or town have a subway? _____

5 What furniture do they have?

A Answer the questions about the pictures.

1. **A:** Do they have a rug?
   B: _Yes, they do._
2. **A:** Do they need a table?
   B: _____
3. **A:** Do they have chairs?
   B: _____
4. **A:** Do they need a dresser?
   B: _____
5. **A:** Do they have a mirror?
   B: _____
6. **A:** Do they have curtains?
   B: _____

7. **A:** Does he have a bookcase?
   B: _____
8. **A:** Does he need curtains?
   B: _____
9. **A:** Does he need a sofa?
   B: _____
10. **A:** Does he have a chair?
    B: _____
11. **A:** Does he have a lamp?
    B: _____
12. **A:** Does he need pictures?
    B: _____

B What furniture do you have? What furniture do you need? Write four sentences.

1. _____
2. _____
3. _____
4. _____

Does it have a view?

6 Complete the description with 's, are, or aren't.

In Martin's apartment, there's_____ a big living room. There _____ two bedrooms and two bathrooms. There _____ no elevator, but there _____ stairs. He has a lot of books, so there _____ bookcases in the living room and bedrooms. There _____ any chairs in the kitchen, but there _____ a big table with chairs in the dining room. There _____ no coffee maker in the kitchen, but there _____ a microwave oven. There _____ two televisions in Martin's apartment – there _____ one television in the living room, and there _____ one television in the bedroom.

7 Answer these questions with information about your home. Use the phrases in the box.

there are no . . .	there isn't a . . .
there are some . . .	there's a . . .
there aren't any . . .	there's no . . .

1. Does your kitchen have a microwave?
   Yes, there's a microwave in my kitchen.
   No, there isn't a microwave. / No, there's no microwave.

2. Does your kitchen have a stove?
   _____

3. Do you have a sofa in your living room?
   _____

4. Do you have bookcases in your living room?
   _____

5. Does your bathroom have a clock?
   _____

6. Do you have pictures in your bedroom?
   _____

7. Does your bedroom have a closet?
   _____

8 What's wrong with this house?

A Write sentences about the house. Use *there* and the words in parentheses.

1. <u>There is no stove in the kitchen. / There isn't a stove in the kitchen.</u> (stove / kitchen)
2. _____ (chairs / dining room)
3. _____ (stove / living room)
4. _____ (refrigerator / bedroom)
5. _____ (bed / bedroom)
6. _____ (armchairs / bathroom)
7. _____ (bed / kitchen)
8. _____ (bookcases / living room)

B Write four more sentences about the house.

1. _____
2. _____
3. _____
4. _____

Does it have a view?

9 Choose the correct responses.

1. **A:** My apartment has a view of the park.
   B: _You're lucky._
   - Guess what!
   - You're lucky.

2. **A:** Do you need living room furniture?
   B: _____
   - Yes, I do. I need a sofa and a coffee table.
   - No, I don't. I need a sofa and a coffee table.

3. **A:** I really need a new desk.
   B: _____
   - So let's go shopping this weekend.
   - That's great!

4. **A:** Do you have chairs in your kitchen?
   B: _____
   - Yes, I do. I need six chairs.
   - Yes, I do. I have six chairs.

10 Draw a picture of your home. Then write a description. Use the questions in the box for ideas.

| Do you live in a house or an apartment? | What rooms does your home have? |
| What furniture do you have? | Who lives with you? |

Unit 7

8 Where do you work?

1 Match these jobs with the correct pictures.

1. lawyer __c__

2. photographer ____

3. bellhop ____

4. police officer ____

5. pilot ____

6. nurse ____

7. server ____

8. salesperson ____

9. cashier ____

10. front desk clerk ____

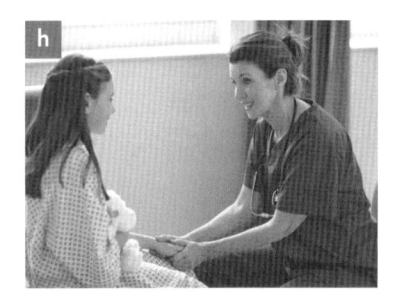

2 What do these people do? Write three sentences about each person. Use the phrases in the box and your own ideas.

| handle food | help people | wear a uniform | work inside |
| handle money | sit / stand all day | work hard | work outside |

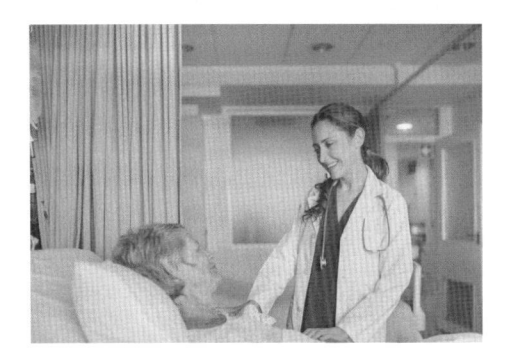

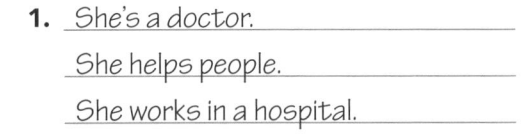

1. She's a doctor.
   She helps people.
   She works in a hospital.

2. _____

3. _____

4. _____

5. _____

6. _____

44 Unit 8

3 **Complete the questions in these conversations.**

1. **A:** Where _does your sister work_?
   B: My sister? She works in a restaurant.
   A: What _does she do_?
   B: She works in the kitchen. She's a chef.

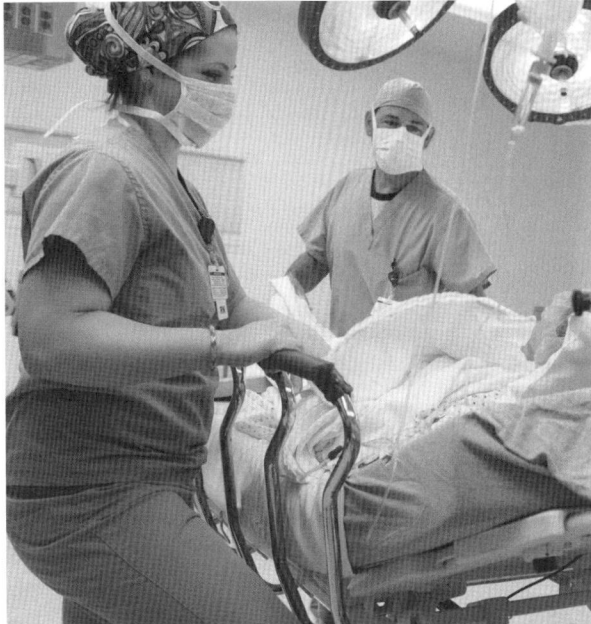

2. **A:** What _____?
   B: Victoria and Jon are nurses. And they work together, too.
   A: Where _____?
   B: At Springfield Hospital.

3. **A:** Where _____?
   B: My daughter works in an office.
   A: What _____?
   B: She's an accountant.

4. **A:** What _____?
   B: Don and I? We're software engineers.
   A: How _____?
   B: We like it a lot!

Where do you work? **45**

4 Complete the conversations.

1. **A:** _____Do_____ you _____have_____ a job?
   B: Yes, I _____ .
   A: Oh, what _____ you _____ ?
   B: I _____ a graphic designer.
   A: Where _____ you _____ ?
   B: I _____ at home.
   A: Oh, wow! How _____ you _____ your job?
   B: I really _____ it. It's a great job!
   A: What time _____ you start work?
   B: I _____ work at 8:00 A.M., and I _____ at 3:00 P.M.

2. **A:** My brother _____ a new job.
   B: Really? Where _____ he _____ ?
   A: He _____ at the Town Center Mall.
   B: What _____ he _____ there?
   A: He _____ a security guard.
   B: How _____ he _____ his job?
   A: Oh, I guess he _____ it.
   B: What time _____ he _____ work?
   A: He _____ work at 10:00 A.M., and he _____ at 6:00 P.M.

5 Exciting or boring?

A Match the adjectives.

1. __d__ exciting
2. _____ easy
3. _____ relaxing
4. _____ safe

a. not stressful
b. not difficult
c. not dangerous
d. not boring

B Write each sentence two different ways.

1. An actor's job is exciting.
   An actor has an exciting job.
   An actor doesn't have a boring job.

2. A security guard has a boring job.
   _____
   _____

3. Paul's job is dangerous.
   _____
   _____

4. A front desk clerk's job is stressful.
   _____
   _____

5. Amanda has a small apartment.
   _____
   _____

6. Cristina's house is big.
   _____
   _____

7. Brenda has a talkative brother.
   _____
   _____

8. My job is easy.
   _____
   _____

Where do you work? **47**

6 Write sentences with your opinion about each job.

1. athlete
2. mechanic 
3. artist 
4. scientist 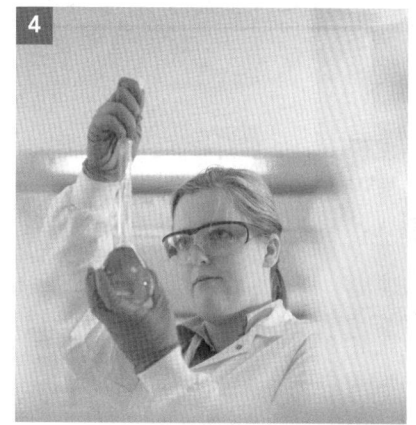
5. plumber 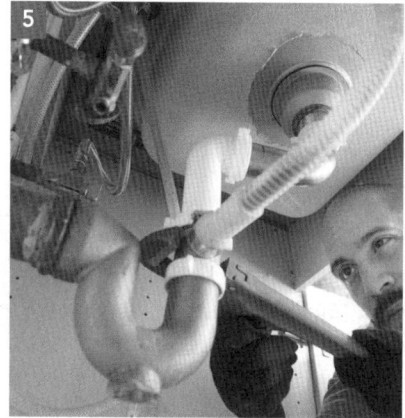
6. reporter 

1. <u>An athlete has an exciting job. / An athlete's job isn't boring.</u>
2. _____
3. _____
4. _____
5. _____
6. _____

7 Imagine you have a dream job. Write a description. Use the questions in the box for ideas.

| What's the job? | What do you do, exactly? |
| Where do you work? | What's the job like? (Is it dangerous, relaxing, or . . . ?) |

_____
_____
_____
_____